Wildlife Wonders

Visit some animal tricksters, rarities, and homebodies

ENCYCLOPÆDIA

Britannica®

CHICAGO　LONDON　NEW DELHI　PARIS　SEOUL　SYDNEY　TAIPEI　TOKYO

Wildlife Wonders

I N T R O D U C T I O N

What kind of bears aren't really bears? What's inside a camel's hump?
Will a mongoose and a cobra ever be friends?
Where would you find a platypus?

In *Wildlife Wonders,* you'll discover answers to these questions and many more. Through pictures, articles, and fun facts, you'll encounter amazing animals, study their actions, and learn how their habitats have changed over time.

To help you on your journey, we've provided the following guideposts in *Wildlife Wonders:*

■ **Subject Tabs**—The colored box in the upper corner of each right-hand page will quickly tell you the article subject.

■ **Search Lights**—Try these mini-quizzes before and after you read the article and see how much—*and how quickly*—you can learn. You can even make this a game with a reading partner. (Answers are upside down at the bottom of one of the pages.)

■ **Did You Know?**—Check out these fun facts about the article subject. With these surprising "factoids," you can entertain your friends, impress your teachers, and amaze your parents.

■ **Picture Captions**—Read the captions that go with the photos. They provide useful information about the article subject.

■ **Vocabulary**—New or difficult words are in **bold type**. You'll find them explained in the Glossary at the end of the book.

■ **Learn More!**—Follow these pointers to related articles in the book. These articles are listed in the Table of Contents and appear on the Subject Tabs.

Britannica

LEARNING
L I B R A R Y

Have a great trip!

The chameleon belongs to a group of reptiles called lizards. Chameleons are known for the ability to change the color of their skin.

Wildlife Wonders

TABLE OF CONTENTS

© Paul A. Souders/Corbis

DID YOU KNOW?

The common nine-banded armadillo is used in studies of the disease leprosy. Armadillos are some of the only animals besides humans that get the disease. And the organism that causes leprosy can't be grown in laboratories.

The Armored Animals

Can you imagine an animal covered in armor from head to toe, like a **medieval** knight? Meet the armadillo. The word "armadillo" means "little armored one" in Spanish.

Armadillos are round creatures with short legs and are about the size of a small dog. They have strong curved claws, and yes, their bodies are covered with armor. Their armor is made of hard plates or scales connected

Armadillo of the Andes Mountains in South America.
© Galen Rowell/Corbis

by bands that stretch. If they didn't stretch, the armadillo would have a hard time moving about.

This armor helps protect the armadillo from its enemies. But its main job is to keep the armadillo from getting cut and scratched by the thorns and cactus that live where it lives.

Central and South America are home to many kinds of armadillos. There you'll find the pichi armadillo, Burmeister's armadillo, and the pink fairy armadillo. You'll also find the giant armadillo, which is nearly five feet long. One **species**, the nine-banded armadillo, is found in Texas and several other U.S. states.

Armadillos can't see very well and are almost toothless. They hunt mostly at night and eat insects and worms, soft roots and fruits, and dead animals that they sometimes find.

When enemies turn up, the armadillo usually runs away into the tough underbrush where its **predators** can't follow. Sometimes the armadillo will jump straight into the air to scare its enemies. As a last resort it will roll itself up into a hard ball.

You may not believe it, but armadillos are also very good swimmers. They stay afloat by swallowing a lot of air. It turns out that under all that armor armadillos are full of surprises!

LEARN MORE! READ THESE ARTICLES...
OPOSSUMS • PORCUPINES • TAPIRS

SEARCH LIGHT

Fill in the blanks: The word "armadillo" is Spanish for "_____ _____ _____."

The long-nosed armadillo is one of South America's many varieties.
© Martin Harvey–Gallo Images/Corbis

Answer: The word "armadillo" is Spanish for "little armored one."

7

SEARCH LIGHT

What's wrong with the following statement: Chameleons can make their skin color change in order to match their surroundings.

The Color-Wizard Lizards

Many people believe that the lizards known as "chameleons" can make their color change to match their surroundings. It's true that the color of a chameleon's skin can change, but not because the chameleon decides to. The color change may help the chameleon avoid its enemies. The color change is a form of **camouflage**, a disguise that lets something blend in with its surroundings.

Chameleon skin contains color-causing substances called "pigments" that change under certain conditions. For instance, on a day when there is no bright sunlight, chameleons appear gray or green. Bright sunlight causes the skin to darken. On cool nights the color fades to a creamy color. The skin also changes color when chameleons are excited, angry, or afraid.

Chameleon of South Africa.
© Erice Reisinger–Gallo Images/Corbis

There are many types of chameleons. About half are found only in the African island of Madagascar. The others occur mostly south of Africa's Sahara desert, with another few in western Asia and southern Europe. The "false chameleon," or anole, is often sold in pet stores. This lizard of the Americas changes color, but not as dramatically as a true chameleon.

Chameleons live in trees, where they usually eat insects. They catch their prey with the help of their long and slender tongue. They shoot the tongue out, grab the prey on the sticky end, and then draw the tongue back into the mouth. Very large chameleons may even use their sticky tongues to catch birds.

Another unusual thing about chameleons is that each eye can move independently of the other, so they can see in different directions at once. This makes it very hard to sneak up on a chameleon.

LEARN MORE! READ THESE ARTICLES…
KING COBRAS • LEMURS • OCELOTS

DID YOU KNOW?

Some say that the chameleon's eyes helped inspire the invention of the military turret, a revolving tower. You can see turrets today on the tops of tanks.

The Parson's chameleon, from Madagascar, is one of the largest of its family.
© Royalty-Free/Corbis

Answer: Chameleons' skin color does change. But they don't decide to change it, and it doesn't always change in order to match their surroundings.

Reptile Royalty

The king cobra is the world's largest poisonous snake. It may grow to twice the length of a Ping-Pong table. Its **venom** is so powerful that elephants have died within three hours of a bite on the toe or trunk.

King cobras are yellow-olive to brownish black, sometimes with lighter bands across the back. Like other cobras, the king cobra is known for its unique "threat display." When it is angered or disturbed, it raises its head and **flares** its narrow, unmarked hood. This shows its yellow or red throat, which often is striped.

The king cobra can raise its head to a third of its entire length and may even move forward while upright. It is very curious by nature and often sits upright to see farther. It may be the most intelligent of all snakes.

The king cobra prowls in forests, fields, and villages. It mostly eats other snakes and normally does not bite humans. In **captivity** it is aggressive to strangers but recognizes its keeper and knows when it's mealtime. However, it can become dangerous during the mating season or when cornered or startled.

The female cobra builds a nest for egg laying. Using a loop of her body as an arm, she pulls leaves, soil, and ground litter into a mound. In this nest she lays 20 to 40 eggs. She coils above or near the eggs for about two months and fiercely defends them.

The king cobra is found in parts of Asia from southern China to the Philippines, Indonesia, and India.

LEARN MORE! READ THESE ARTICLES...
ELEPHANTS • MONGOOSES • SPIDERS

SEARCH LIGHT

People are afraid of cobras and as a result often kill the snakes. Why do you think people are scared of cobras? (Hint: What would you worry about if you came face to face with a cobra?)

DID YOU KNOW?

The king cobra has an unusual hiss that is much lower than other snakes'—more like a growl than a hiss.

The king cobra (like other cobras) performs the famous "threat display" by pulling the ribs of the neck sideways and forward. This flattens the neck into a hood.
© E. Hanumantha Rao/NHPA

Answer: Because cobras are poisonous and have occasionally killed people with their bite, many consider the snake a danger to humans. Cobras also have a flaring "hood" that makes them look threatening. Actually, far more snakes are injured and killed by people each year than the other way around.

DID YOU KNOW?
Unlike their cousins the housecats, ocelots don't mind a swim now and then. They're quite good at it!

Spotted American Cats

When we think of cats, we usually think of small housecats or big cats like lions and tigers. But there are many kinds of cats of all sizes that still live in the wild. One such cat is the ocelot. The ocelot is about twice the size of a housecat.

Ocelot of Costa Rica, in Central America.
© Kevin Schafer/Corbis

The ocelot is found in the Western Hemisphere, from Texas in the southwestern United States down to Argentina in South America. It lives in several different habitats, including tropical forests, grasslands, and brush.

The ocelot's fur is short, smooth, and yellowish gray. There are small black spots on its head, two black stripes on each cheek, and four or five black stripes along its neck. This coat is good **camouflage** for the ocelot. It makes the animal hard to see in the leafy shade, for example. But its patterned fur is also attractive to humans. People hunt the ocelot for its fur, and so the number of ocelots in the wild has shrunk. In the United States, it's illegal to hunt ocelots or to sell their fur.

In the wild, ocelots generally like to live alone. They sleep during the day, usually in a tree or in other heavy plant cover. At night they hunt for rodents, birds, reptiles, and fish. However, they will also kill pets and other small **domestic** animals left outdoors.

Ocelot kittens start hunting with their mothers when they are about three months old. When they are a year old, they leave the mother and start living on their own.

Some people try to keep ocelots as pets, since they are easily tamed when they're kittens. But when they grow up, the adult ocelots can sometimes be bad-tempered.

LEARN MORE! READ THESE ARTICLES...
CHAMELEONS • LIONS • OPOSSUMS

SEARCH LIGHT

Look at the small photo. Why do you think it's hard to know just how many ocelots there are in some areas? (Hint: What do the spots on the ocelot's fur do for it?)

Answer: Ocelots sleep during the day in trees and other areas with dense leaf cover. An ocelot's spotted coat helps it blend into a leafy background and makes it difficult to see, day or night.

13

SEARCH LIGHT

How many babies can a mother opossum carry in her pouch at one time?

DID YOU KNOW?
People often picture opossums hanging from tree branches by their tails. Although they wrap them around branches to help keep their balance, opossums don't actually hang by their tails.

Playing Dead to Stay Alive

Have you ever been out at night and come across a gray creature about the size of a housecat, with a long, pointy white face and beady little eyes? If so, you've probably met an opossum.

Opossums are marsupials, which are mammals that carry their young in pouches on their bellies. Like kittens and puppies, baby opossums are born blind. So the first thing they do is snuggle inside their mother's built-in belly pouch. About 13 baby opossums can fit and feed inside the pouch at one time. They stay in there and go everywhere with the mother.

An opossum "playing possum."
© Joe McDonald/Corbis

While they're in the pouch, the tiny opossums grow until they are the size of little mice. Then, after five weeks, they crawl out and ride piggyback on the mother's back. They hold on to her thick silvery-black fur with special grabbing thumbs.

Loaded with babies on her back, as the large photo shows, the mother opossum scampers through the woods and scurries up trees. She scrambles through bushes looking for fruits and berries. She climbs trees to find insects, birds' eggs, and little creatures to eat. When one of the babies gets tired, it just tumbles back into the pouch for a rest.

Opossums—or "possums," as they're sometimes called—have another strange behavior. Most **predatory** animals like to eat live food and will lose interest in animals that are already dead. So the opossum sometimes escapes its enemies by pretending to be dead. It will freeze like a statue and then topple over to the ground. When the predator loses interest and leaves, the opossum calmly gets up and walks away. This clever trick has become known as "playing possum."

LEARN MORE! READ THESE ARTICLES…
ARMADILLOS • KANGAROOS • LEMURS

Touch Me Nots

The porcupine's name comes from words meaning "pig" and "spines." This small rodent's body is covered with dark fur and the sharp quills, or spines, that give it its name. Some porcupine quills are attached in bunches, and others are attached singly. But all quills are used to protect against enemies.

Baby New World porcupine.
© D. Robert & Lorri Franz/Corbis

Porcupines can't actually shoot their quills through the air. When it's threatened, a porcupine puffs out its quills. The quills easily come loose if touched and stick in an enemy's skin. They can cause painful wounds and may kill if they make their way into vital organs or cause infection.

There are 25 **species** of porcupines, divided into Old World and New World porcupines.

Old World porcupines include the **crested** porcupines of Africa, Asia, and Europe. Long-tailed porcupines are also found in Asia. Brush-tailed porcupines are found in Asia and Africa.

The best-known New World species is the forest-dwelling North American porcupine. Other species found in the tropical forests from Mexico to South America use their long tails to grab onto branches. Porcupines shelter in tree branches and roots, hollow logs, burrows, and caves. Old World species like to stay on the ground more than New World porcupines do.

Porcupines are most active at night. They eat almost any tree part they can reach, including the bark. North American porcupines prefer a tender layer beneath the bark. In trying to get at it, they may chew away the bark in a ring, which kills the tree. Porcupines sometimes gnaw antlers and wooden tools such as ax handles and canoe paddles for the salt and oil they contain.

LEARN MORE! READ THESE ARTICLES...
ARMADILLOS • OPOSSUMS • TAPIRS

SEARCH LIGHT

Why do you think an ax handle would have salt in it that a porcupine would want?

DID YOU KNOW?
Baby porcupines have very soft quills when they're born, kind of like cooked spaghetti. The quills stiffen quickly after the baby is born.

Old World porcupines like this one have quills embedded in clusters. New World porcupines have quills interspersed with hair, underfur, and bristles.

© Vittoriano Rastelli/Corbis

Answer: People sweat through their hands when they work. An ax handle would soak up the sweat as well as the salt in the sweat.

DID YOU KNOW?

Although the gibbon's thumb helps it swing through the trees, it's a problem in other ways. The thumb is so far from the other fingers that the gibbon can't use it to control tools as a chimpanzee can.

The Swinging Singers

A gibbon is in the family of apes, but it is a "lesser ape." That's because it's smaller and less intelligent than such great apes as the chimpanzee and gorilla.

Gibbons are found in the tropical rainforests of Southeast Asia. There the gibbon uses its long arms to swing from branch to branch in the jungle's thick **canopy**. Its long, thin hands and feet help make the gibbon a very good **aerialist**. The gibbon's thumb starts from the wrist, and not the palm of its hand. This means the thumb acts like a hook on branches. The gibbon's feet also have a long split between the big toe and the other toes. This split provides a firm foothold on branches.

Because they are well suited for tree climbing, gibbons spend most of their time traveling along branches. And they don't have to leave the trees for dinner. They eat fruit, leaves, vegetables, and insects, all of which are found in the canopy.

White-handed gibbon, also called Malayan lar.
© Tom McHugh/Photo Researchers

Gibbons live in small family groups of a male, a female, and their young. The male and female "sing" in the morning and evening, and the males sometimes give solo performances. Gibbons are **territorial**, and singing lets everyone know that they are at home. The moment the family home is threatened, gibbons will hoot and leap and swing excitedly.

Gibbons are a great attraction at zoos because they're such fun to watch. Unfortunately, in the natural world they are in danger of disappearing altogether.

LEARN MORE! READ THESE ARTICLES...
APES • GORILLAS • LEMURS

The gray gibbon lives on the island of Borneo in Southeast Asia.
© Uwe Walz/Corbis

Answer: When gibbons sing, it lets other gibbons know where they are.

DID YOU KNOW?
Koko is a gorilla that has learned some basic American Sign Language. Not everyone agrees that she is actually communicating, but most agree that she has a large sign-language vocabulary.

Fierce but Shy Apes

SEARCH LIGHT

Although gorillas look **ferocious**, they are really very quiet and shy. They live in family groups in the thickest parts of jungles, where they are not likely to be disturbed. At night, the father gorilla sleeps on the ground while the mother and the baby gorillas sleep in big nests of sticks and leaves. Sometimes they sleep in the lower branches of trees, where they are safe from **prowling** animals.

If you were to visit a gorilla's home, the male head of the group would take steps to protect his family. The first step would be to beat his chest, grunt, hoot, and roar in order to scare you away. Rather than fighting you, the gorilla would hope that you left on your own.

Why do you think people would make the mistake of thinking that gorillas are naturally fierce? (Hint: Look at the face of the gorilla in the large photo.)

Mountain gorilla family in Rwanda.
© Yann Arthus-Bertrand/Corbis

A gorilla's feet, hands, and wrinkled face are bare and black. Its arms are so long they almost touch the ground, even when it is standing up. A gorilla's fur may be short or long, depending on where it lives. The short-haired gorilla lives in the hot, damp jungles of western Africa. The long-haired gorilla lives in the cooler high mountains of central Africa. There are not many gorillas of either kind left in the wild.

Gorillas and chimpanzees are the closest living animal "relatives" to humans. Along with the bonobos and the orangutans, these animals make up the "great apes." Like the other great apes, gorillas are very clever and can solve problems. They have good memories, and some can even learn sign language. You never know, someday you may sit down and have a chat with our cousin the gorilla!

LEARN MORE! READ THESE ARTICLES...
APES · GIBBONS · PANDAS

A male mountain gorilla like this one may weigh as much as 400 pounds. Females are smaller at up to about 200 pounds.
© Kennan Ward/Corbis

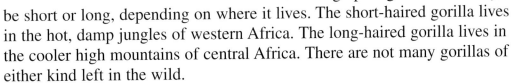

Answer: When we see someone with a heavy brow, we usually suppose that person is frowning and angry. People who aren't used to seeing gorillas often think that the gorillas' expressions mean they have the same feelings as people.

Meet the King and Queen of Beasts

Unlike all other big cats, lions live in groups, called "prides." Prides of lions can be found in grasslands, desert areas, and rocky hills. But except for African animal parks, there are not many places left in the world where lions still run free. Today the only wild lions outside Africa are a few hundred protected in the Gir Forest National Park of northwestern India.

Each pride is made up of lionesses (female lions) of different ages, all of which are related, plus their cubs and one or two adult male lions. A pride may have as few as 4 or as many as 37 members. But about 15 is the usual size.

During the day lions lie in the shade or climb trees and rest on the branches. But lions become very active at night. Like other cats, they can see well in dim light and like to hunt in the dark. Lions hunt grazing animals, such as zebras, antelope, buffalo, and gazelles.

Male lion.
© Randy Wells/Corbis

Most lions will not attack a human or a large animal such as a giraffe or a hippopotamus. Those that live near a village may carry away donkeys, goats, or even small cows. Imagine how strong a lion's teeth and neck have to be to lift a cow over a fence!

Male lions are usually identified by their big fur collars called "manes" and by the dark **tuft** of hair on their tails. Females are the same sandy color as males, but they are a little smaller. Lion cubs have dark spots when they are born.

You may think lions only roar, but they also growl, grunt, and cough. Sometimes they even purr like giant pussycats.

LEARN MORE! READ THESE ARTICLES…
ELEPHANTS · GAZELLES · OCELOTS

SEARCH LIGHT

The male lion in the smaller photo has a big shaggy mane. Why do you think male lions have manes? (Hint: Male lions guard and protect the pride's territory.)

Female lions such as these do most of the hunting.
The males usually roar to "scare up" the prey while
the females lie in wait.
© Tom Brakefield/Corbis

Answer: A male lion has to look fierce and strong to scare off other animals. The mane makes him look bigger and scarier.

The gray wolf is also known as the "timber wolf." In spite of its name, the gray wolf may be brown, reddish, black, or whitish on its back.

© Tom Brakefield/Corbis

SEARCH LIGHT

Fill in the blank. The alpha male and female are the pack

_____.

Noble Hunters, Strong Families

Wolves are very intelligent animals. They are also quite social, living and hunting in family packs. They have a strict ranking system, with a **dominant** female and male—the alpha pair—leading the pack. Only the alpha pair mate and have puppies, though the whole pack helps raise the young. Four to seven pups are born at a time.

Packs have 7 to 30 members, depending on how much **prey** is available. Each pack patrols a home territory of 40 to more than 400 square miles. They define their territory with scent markings and with growls, barks, and their legendary howls.

Adult gray wolves and cub.
© Tom Brakefield/Corbis

Even though they're not terribly fast, wolves are excellent hunters. They tackle much larger animals and can even bring down huge moose and bison. Usually they hunt caribou and elk, but they might even eat mice if that's all they can find.

Wolves hunt by using their keen senses and group cooperation. They work by tiring out their prey, sometimes chasing it all night. At the end they encircle their prey, waiting for the chance to attack unexpectedly. As soon as the animal has been brought down, the pack will feed. The highest-ranking members eat first and get all the tastiest bits.

Wolves belong to the canine family. Their relatives include jackals, coyotes, dingoes, New Guinea singing dogs, wild dogs of Africa, and the **domestic** dogs people keep as pets.

Scientists believe that wolves may be the original canine from which the others descended. However, only three **species** of wolves remain today. There are gray wolves in Europe, Asia, Canada, Alaska, and Yellowstone Park (U.S.). A few hundred Ethiopian wolves live in a small part of Africa. Red wolves now survive mostly in **captivity**, but they used to roam the southeastern United States.

LEARN MORE! READ THESE ARTICLES…
APES • LIONS • OCELOTS

Answer: The alpha male and female are the pack leaders.

SEARCH LIGHT

Fill in the blank. Koalas are marsupials, which means they nurse and carry their babies in a

_____

on their bellies.

The Bears That Aren't Really Bears

This roly-poly little animal has shiny black eyes that look like wet licorice candy. Its funny black nose is pressed against its face between bushy gray ears. If you found this animal in your bedroom, you might think it was a toy teddy bear.

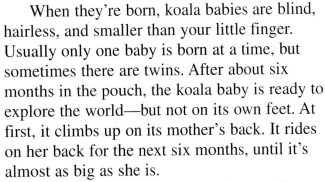

DID YOU KNOW?
Koalas are often slow-moving and quiet. Some people believe that their eucalyptus diet has a calming effect on them. The truth is, however, that their digestion rate is slowed down because the leaves take a lot of energy to digest.

But this is a real animal (though it isn't a real bear) called the koala. It is found only in Australia. The koala drinks dew and eats nothing but leaves of the eucalyptus tree, as shown in the large photo. It is famously slow-moving and gentle, and it sleeps up to 16 hours a day. Even when they're being **aggressive**, koalas rarely use their energy to fight. Instead, they'll make loud croaking sounds known as "bellowing."

Koalas are related to kangaroos. Both are marsupials. Marsupial mothers carry and nurse their young in a pouch on their bellies. It's like a built-in baby basket.

Mother koala carrying baby on her back.
© David and Eric Hosking/Corbis

When they're born, koala babies are blind, hairless, and smaller than your little finger. Usually only one baby is born at a time, but sometimes there are twins. After about six months in the pouch, the koala baby is ready to explore the world—but not on its own feet. At first, it climbs up on its mother's back. It rides on her back for the next six months, until it's almost as big as she is.

Mothers and babies communicate with gentle squeaks, clicks, and hums. A grunt indicates irritation or impatience. After a year the young koala leaves its mother to make its own home. Koalas are very **territorial**, and the young are not encouraged to hang around once they can take care of themselves.

LEARN MORE! READ THESE ARTICLES...
KANGAROOS • PANDAS • PLATYPUSES

Answer: Koalas are marsupials, which means they nurse and carry their babies in a pouch on their bellies.

Snakes' Feared Rivals

Curled up in its soft burrow, the shaggy-haired mongoose looks gentle and harmless. But when it's hungry, a mongoose is a very dangerous creature. Some people call the mongoose "furred lightning" because it can move faster than a snake can strike. This makes the mongoose the most famous snake killer in the world.

There are over 40 species of mongoose living in Asia, Africa, and Europe. India is home to both the mongoose and the cobra, a highly poisonous snake. When a mongoose meets a cobra, the mongoose uses its speed and sharp teeth to grab the snake behind the head. Then it hits the cobra against the ground until the snake is dead.

Yellow mongoose, also called meerkat.
© Martin Harvey–Gallo Images/Corbis

Because of their snake-fighting ways, mongooses are very welcome in places where there are many poisonous snakes. Sometimes people in these places keep mongooses as pets. But mongooses aren't allowed in most countries of the world, not even to be kept in zoos. It is dangerous to bring even a few mongooses into a country where they do not naturally live.

Some countries have made the mistake of **importing** mongooses to help kill snakes and rats. The problem is that once the mongooses have killed and eaten most of the snakes and rats, they still need food. So the mongooses hunt the other small animals that they can catch, and they can catch almost anything. No bird, rabbit, squirrel, or chipmunk is safe from the "terror of the fields." Few animals are quick enough to escape a hungry mongoose.

LEARN MORE! READ THESE ARTICLES…
KING COBRAS • PORCUPINES • WOLVES

SEARCH LIGHT

Can you tell from the large picture how a mongoose keeps from getting bitten by snakes? (Hint: The snake's tail is still on the ground.)

This yellow mongoose in Botswana has just won its battle with a snake.
© Gallo Images/Corbis

Answer: The mongoose grabs the snake just behind the head so that the snake can't reach it with its fangs.

Cuddly Exotic Bears

When you think of pandas, you probably picture a big cuddly black-and-white bear. But there are actually two kinds of pandas: the giant panda and the lesser panda. The giant panda is the familiar black-and-white animal, which is found mostly in the forests of China and Tibet. The lesser panda looks rather like a raccoon.

The giant panda grows to about 5 feet long and 220 pounds. Its favorite food is bamboo, and it eats almost nothing else. It needs to consume large quantities of bamboo to get the nourishment that its body needs, so it spends about 10 to 12 hours a day eating. **Captive** pandas, like those found in zoos, have a broader diet. In addition to bamboo, they may eat cereals, milk, and garden vegetables.

Lesser panda.
© Keren Su/Corbis

The lesser panda is smaller and has rich reddish brown fur on its back and black fur on its belly. It has a bushy ringed tail that makes it look a little like a raccoon. The lesser panda is sometimes called a "cat bear" or "red bear cat." It's also found in China, as well as in the South Asian countries of Myanmar, Nepal, and India. Like its giant cousin, the lesser panda also eats bamboo. But it also eats grasses, fruits, other plant material, and, sometimes, small animals.

Giant pandas are endangered animals. Their natural habitat keeps shrinking each year. But many countries are trying to help China preserve its bamboo forests so that pandas have a place to live. People are also working to increase the number of pandas by breeding them in zoos.

LEARN MORE! READ THESE ARTICLES...
GORILLAS · KOALAS · YAKS

There are probably only about 1,000 giant pandas left in the wild. Another 100 or so live in zoos.
© Keren Su/Corbis

SEARCH LIGHT

In the wild, giant pandas get most of their food from bamboo plants. What will happen if people in China keep cutting down the bamboo forests?

DID YOU KNOW?

Many people call the panda a panda bear, but for a long time scientists weren't sure if it really *was* a bear. Today, in spite of some non-bear traits, the panda is usually classified in the bear family.

Answer: If people continue to cut down the bamboo forests, then giant pandas will starve and die out. They simply couldn't adjust to a life without bamboo.

Intelligent Creatures ...Like Us!

Apes are the most humanlike of all animals. Like people, apes do their work during the day and sleep at night. They also live in families and communities like we do. And like humans, apes sometimes fight each other. Great apes, like humans, can learn to use tools.

In the wild, some of the apes known as "chimpanzees" use twigs and leaves as tools. They cleverly poke a twig inside the nests of ants and termites. Then they pull up the twig and eat the insects that cling to it. They make leaf cups to scoop up water. They also use leaves and twigs to clean themselves.

There are two types of apes: great apes and lesser apes. The great apes include orangutans, gorillas, chimpanzees, and bonobos. The lesser apes include gibbons and siamangs. Apes live mostly in the tropical forests of Africa and Asia. The orangutan, whose name means "person of the forest," is found today only on the islands of Borneo and Sumatra.

Why do you think that the ability to learn to make and use tools may indicate intelligence? (Hint: What do tools help you do?)

Family of chimpanzees.
© Paul A. Souders/Corbis

Gibbons and orangutans live in trees. Chimpanzees and bonobos live in trees and on the ground. Gorillas spend most of their time on the ground but sometimes sleep in trees. Most apes like to eat shoots, fruits, leaves, seeds, and grass. But while most apes will eat insects, little birds, birds' eggs, rodents, and other young animals, gorillas don't eat meat at all.

Chimpanzees and gorillas are intelligent animals. Scientists have even taught some of them to solve problems and use sign language.

Can you guess what the most noticeable physical difference between an ape and a monkey is? Apes don't have tails! And they don't have claws either. They have flat nails like we do.

LEARN MORE! READ THESE ARTICLES...
GIBBONS • GORILLAS • LEMURS

Orangutans, such as these from Sumatra, are among the group called the "great apes." Great apes are considerably more intelligent than the "lesser apes" (gibbons).
© Tom Brakefield/Corbis

Answer: Tools help animals—including people—control and change their environment. Many animals have adapted to their surroundings in amazing ways. But very few besides apes and humans are able to make their surroundings adapt to them.

33

Fliers by Night

Bats are mammals, and like all mammals they have fur, give birth to live babies, and feed their babies milk. But bats are also the only **mammals** that truly fly.

Bats live all over the world, but they prefer warm climates. They like to live in huge groups, or colonies, sometimes with 1,000 bats or more in a colony. Bats sleep in caves, the hollows of trees, and empty buildings.

There are many kinds of bats, in many sizes. The flying fox bat, when it stretches its wings, is wider than you are tall. But the tiny Philippine bamboo bat's wings are barely six inches from tip to tip.

Most bats eat insects. The Mexican bats of Texas can eat up millions and millions of insects every year! Other bats eat fruits, honey, and **pollen**. But whatever they eat, all bats look for their food at night.

You may have heard the term "blind as a bat." Bats actually see very clearly, but they don't rely on their eyes. When a bat flies, it makes a sound that we can't hear. That sound bounces off objects in the bat's path, creating an echo its large ears can hear. Those echoes tell the bat what's ahead of it and help it locate food or enemies.

(Top) Leaf-nosed bat; (bottom) fruit bat.

Some people fear bats, but in fact they are very helpful. Not only do they eat insects that pester us, but bats also help **pollinate** many flowers and plants. Without bats many plants, such as some kinds of cactus, wouldn't be alive.

LEARN MORE! READ THESE ARTICLES...
OCELOTS • OSTRICHES • PLATYPUSES

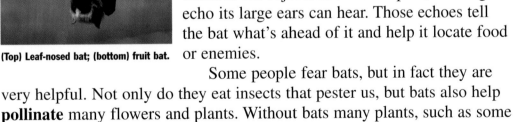

SEARCH LIGHT

True or false? Bats are solitary animals.

Answer: FALSE. Bats live in huge groups, or colonies.

The Silk Spinners

SEARCH LIGHT

How does the pirate spider catch its food?

Spiders belong to a large group of animals called "arthropods." This group also includes crabs, centipedes, and insects. Arthropods have their skeletons on the outside of their bodies.

Though they're part of the same larger group, spiders are not insects. Insects have six legs, while spiders have eight. This makes them part of a smaller group, the arachnids. Arachnids—including **scorpions** and ticks—have eight walking legs. Many spiders and other arachnids use **venom** to kill their prey.

Spiders also spin silk. In fact, the word "spider" comes from an old English word that means "to spin." Spiders have silk-making organs called "spinnerets" near the back of their bodies. They spin silk from a liquid made by special **glands**. It becomes solid thread after the spider pushes it out of its body.

Spiders spin different types of silk for different uses. Some silk is stronger than steel wire. Spiders use silk for webs to trap food, for lining their nests, and to hold the eggs they lay. When a spider has to escape from an enemy, it may quickly spin a getaway thread and drop out of sight on it.

Jumping spider ready to pounce.
© Robert Pickett/Corbis

Not all spiders catch food with a web. Some, such as the jumping spider, pounce like a cat to capture insects. Others spin silk funnels, where they hide during the day before going hunting at night. The brightly colored crab spider hides between flower petals and grabs insects looking for nectar. Pirate spiders creep inside the webs spun by other spiders and then eat them up.

LEARN MORE! READ THESE ARTICLES...
BATS • WILD GOATS

Many spiders spin webs to trap food—most often insects such as this unfortunate butterfly.
© Tecmap Corporation—Eric Curry/Corbis

DID YOU KNOW?

Spiders live everywhere, even underwater. Water spiders are called "diving bells" because they build bell-shaped webs underwater. The bell webs trap air bubbles for the spider to breathe.

Answer: A pirate spider eats other spiders out of their own webs.

SEARCH LIGHT

Fill in
the blank:
The kiwi is an
unusual bird. Its
_____
are not fully formed,
so it does not fly.

New Zealand's Feathered Favorites

The kiwi is a strange little bird found only in the forests of the island nation of New Zealand. During the day it sleeps in its burrow, and at night it looks for food, as the one in the large photo is doing. Kiwis eat worms, insects, **larvae**, spiders, and berries.

Kiwis have a strong sense of smell, which they use to hunt. They are the only birds whose nostrils are on the very tip of the bill. The kiwi's bill is long and narrow. Having their noses at the very end of their bills is a big help when they are hunting!

"Kiwi crossing" road sign in New Zealand.
© Paul A. Souders/Corbis

Kiwis also have a good sense of hearing, though they have poor vision in daylight. To escape enemies they rely on their strong legs. Kiwis are fast runners and fierce fighters. They have four toes on each foot, each with a large claw. The claws are very useful when kiwis are facing enemies.

The kiwi is an unusual bird. It is a grayish brown and about as big as a chicken. It has wings that are not fully formed, so it does not fly. The wings are hidden in its feathers, which are shaggy and hairlike. It also has sensitive whiskers at the base of its bill.

The bird is much loved by the people of New Zealand, even though they don't see it very often. New Zealanders themselves are sometimes called Kiwis. A fruit, a breakfast cereal, and an airline are named after the kiwi too. Pictures of the bird can be seen on New Zealand's postage stamps and coins.

> ### DID YOU KNOW?
> Compared with the size of the bird, the kiwi's egg isn't just large, it's enormous. The egg is about 20 percent of the mother's weight. It fills almost her entire body right before it's laid.

LEARN MORE! READ THESE ARTICLES…
KANGAROOS • OSTRICHES • PLATYPUSES

Answer: The kiwi is an unusual bird. Its wings are not fully formed, so it does not fly.

SEARCH LIGHT

Which of the following can be said about ostriches?
- Ostriches eat a lot of meat.
- Ostriches are the biggest bird.
- Ostriches are great runners.

The Biggest Birds in the World

The ostrich is the largest living bird in the world. Ostriches are about 8 feet tall and may weigh as much as 345 pounds. They have very short wings, which means ostriches are too heavy to fly. Ostriches' wings can't get them into the air, but flapping their wings while they run helps the birds go faster on the ground. Ostriches can run up to 40 miles an hour. This makes them not just the biggest but also the fastest bird on the ground!

Ostriches don't use their speed to catch food. Instead, they run to keep away from their enemies. But the first thing ostriches do when they see an enemy is hide. To avoid being seen, ostriches generally lie flat on the ground with their necks outstretched. This makes them look like just another bush. People sometimes say that ostriches bury their heads in the sand when they sense danger. But this isn't true. You just can't see their heads when ostriches are lying down.

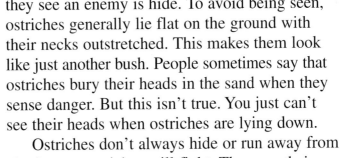

Male ostrich protecting eggs in a nest.
© Kevin Schafer/Corbis

Ostriches don't always hide or run away from trouble. If their babies are in danger, ostriches will fight. They use their beaks, and they kick with their very powerful legs. An ostrich could easily kill a person with a few kicks of its feet.

Wild ostriches live in groups in Africa. Sometimes there are as many as 50 birds in a single group. Ostriches eat mostly plants, fruits, and berries, but once in a while they'll also eat small animals and insects.

A tame ostrich that's been treated well may do a very special thing: it can be trained to carry people on its back. In fact, in some parts of the world people have ostrich races.

LEARN MORE! READ THESE ARTICLES…
GAZELLES • LIONS • OPOSSUMS

DID YOU KNOW?
In the days when fashionable women wore showy hats, they were often decorated with ostrich feathers.

Answer: Ostriches are the biggest bird. Ostriches are great runners.

Egg-Laying Mammals

If someone asked you to describe a mammal, you might say a mammal is a warm-blooded animal with hair or fur. You'd add that mammals give birth to live babies instead of laying eggs and that they feed their young with milk.

Well, the platypus feeds its babies milk. And the platypus is warm-blooded and has brown fur. But the platypus breaks a big mammal rule—it lays eggs. Platypuses and Australian spiny anteaters are the only members of an egg-laying mammal group called "monotremes."

Platypuses are found in the lakes and streams of Tasmania and eastern and southern Australia. They spend their lives feeding along the bottoms of rivers, streams, and lakes and resting in burrows dug into banks.

A platypus has a big appetite. The amount of food it eats every day is almost equal to its own weight. A platypus meal may consist of insects, shellfish, fishes, frogs, **mollusks**, tadpoles, or earthworms.

The platypus often looks for food underwater. But in the water, the platypus's eyes and ears are closed. Since it can't see or hear underwater, the platypus depends entirely on its snout to find its food. But what a snout! The platypus snout looks like a duck's bill, which is why the platypus is sometimes called the "duckbill."

The platypus also has webbed feet like a duck and a tail like a beaver. When you look at it, the platypus doesn't seem to be a single animal but rather appears to be several different animals put together.

LEARN MORE! READ THESE ARTICLES…
KANGAROOS • KIWIS • OPOSSUMS

SEARCH LIGHT

Which of the following statements about the platypus are true?
- It has fur.
- It is warm-blooded.
- It gives birth to live babies.

The platypus, so awkward and peculiar on the ground,
is perfectly adapted for underwater hunting.
© Joe McDonald/Corbis

SEARCH LIGHT

What are three reasons that tapirs are becoming endangered?

This Malayan tapir is related to the horse, but it looks more like a pig. To add to the confusion, its baby is called a "calf," like a cow's baby.
© Kevin Schafer/Corbis

DID YOU KNOW?

It takes about 13 months for a tapir baby to be born. That might seem like a lot to us humans, who take only 9 months. But it's nothing to the elephant, which carries its baby for 24 months.

Shy Cousins of the Horse and Rhino

The tapir is a strange-looking animal. It has a stumpy tail and a soft flexible snout like a short elephant trunk. Some tapirs are brown or gray. Others have a black head and legs, with a dirty-white back and belly. Its feet have hooves, just like a horse.

In fact, tapirs are related to horses, and to rhinos too. You wouldn't know it to look at them, since tapirs don't look much like either animal. But when it's feeding, the tapir uses its nose to move things aside and graze on plants, like a horse does.

South American tapir of Ecuador.
© Michael & Patricia Fogden/Corbis

The shy, **solitary** tapir is found in Myanmar, Malaysia, Thailand, and Sumatra. It also lives in the forests of Central and South America. The tapirs in Central America are the largest, about as big as a donkey.

Tapirs usually live deep in the forest near swamps and rivers. They're good swimmers and often escape from enemies into the water. In South America the tapir's main enemy is the jaguar. In Asia it has to beware of tigers.

But the tapir's greatest enemy, no matter where it lives, is people. Tapirs are endangered, which means their numbers in the wild are decreasing. This is because people cut down forests for wood and clear land to grow crops, destroying the home of the tapir and of many other animals as well. And besides the threat from tigers and jaguars, tapirs also face human hunters who kill them for food and sport.

With luck, people will soon pay more attention to preserving this unusual animal in the wild.

LEARN MORE! READ THESE ARTICLES…
ELEPHANTS • OPOSSUMS • PLATYPUSES

Answer: They are hunted by jaguars and tigers.
They are hunted by people.
People cut down their forest homes.

Packed and Ready to Go

Did you know that a camel's hump is like a lunch box? After a good feed, a camel changes the extra food and water into fat and keeps it safe in its hump. A camel can then go for days without food or water, living on that fat. That is why people use them for crossing deserts. Camels don't have to stop all the time for a drink or a bite to eat.

When camels do get hungry, they're definitely not hard to feed. Camels eat all kinds of grass and plants, even those that are dry and thorny. In fact, a hungry camel will gobble up tents, straw baskets, and even leather belts and will drink 25 gallons of water in just a few minutes!

The dromedary, or Arabian camel, has one hump. You'll find the dromedary in North Africa, the Middle East, and India. The Bactrian camel, which lives mostly in Central Asian countries, has two humps. Both camels can carry people and heavy loads and are excellent for making long journeys. But camels can be quite ill-tempered. They bellow, bite, or kick hard if you tease them. They even spit when they're unhappy!

Camels are useful in other ways too. Their hair is used to make tents, blankets, rugs, ropes, and clothes. Camel skin is used to make footwear and bags. Cheese and other foods are made from camel milk.

Here's an **oddity**: camels have a double set of eyelashes. These help to keep the camel's eyes safe from sand during desert storms. During sandstorms the camel just closes its nose while long hair protects its eyes...and its ears too.

LEARN MORE! READ THESE ARTICLES...
ELEPHANTS · GAZELLES · LLAMAS

SEARCH LIGHT

True or false? Camels store extra food in their humps.

Bactrian camel.
© Corbis

Dromedary, or Arabian camel.
© Jose Fuste Raga/Corbis

DID YOU KNOW?
If a mother camel has to go on a journey when her baby is very young, the baby is put inside a carrier on a "nurse" camel beside the mother. If the mother can't see the baby, she'll run away, perhaps thinking her baby is lost and she needs to find it!

Answer: **TRUE.**

SEARCH LIGHT

An African elephant can weigh as much as
a) a whale.
b) a bus.
c) a big snail.

The Largest Animals on Land

Can you tell an African elephant from an Indian elephant?

First check out the ears: African elephants have much larger ears than Indian elephants. African elephants are larger and stronger and have thicker skin than their Indian cousins. In fact, African elephants are the largest animals on land. They can grow to more than 11 feet tall and 12,000 pounds!

(Top) In Kerala state in India, elephants are respected and honored. During festivals like this, they are dressed in gold faceplates that look like armor. (Bottom) Adult and young African elephants.

Indian elephants, found in South and Southeast Asia, are smaller, gentler, and easier to train. Most elephants in zoos and circuses are Indian. Elephants and people have long worked together. Usually, one man trains one elephant. In India, the trainer is called a *mahout.* In Burma, he is the *oozie.* Both African and Indian elephants have been used in wartime.

Both kinds of elephants eat fruits, nuts, grass, and vegetables, but trees are their favorite food. To get at the tree leaves they like, elephants break off branches with their trunks or sometimes just knock the whole tree down. Elephants also breathe, smell, and trumpet through their trunks. When they're hot, elephants take baths to cool off. They swim underwater and stick their trunks up in the air and breathe through them. Elephants also take showers with their trunks by sucking up water and spraying it on themselves.

Male elephants have huge tusks for digging, carrying things, and sometimes fighting. But their tusks also cause elephants problems. Hunters have killed so many elephants for the ivory in their tusks that there are not many left.

LEARN MORE! READ THESE ARTICLES…
CAMELS · KING COBRAS · TAPIRS

Indian elephants in Sri Lanka.
© Lindsay Hebberd/Corbis

Answer: b) a bus.

Bounty of the
Andes

The llama is closely related to the alpaca, the guanaco, and the vicuña. Altogether these animals are called "lamoids." They are part of the camel family, but lamoids do not have humps like camels.

(Top) Herding llamas in the highlands of Peru; (bottom) Quechua Indian girl with llama.

Llamas are the largest lamoids. They are about 4 feet tall, can weigh 250 pounds, and have long legs and a long neck. Their coat is usually white, but some llamas are black, brown, or white with black markings.

Today most llamas are **domestic animals**. They are kept by South American Indians in the mountains of Bolivia, Peru, Ecuador, Chile, and Argentina. The llama has many uses. It is a source of food and milk. It also provides wool that can be used to make knitted clothing and woven fabrics. Llama hair is also used to weave rugs and rope. Llama **dung** can be dried and used as fuel.

The llama is also an important transport animal. It's strong, and it can go a long time without water. Also, the llama eats many kinds of plants. These traits make the llama perfectly suited for traveling the plateaus and mountains of the Andes, where there is very little water or vegetation. The llamas can carry a 100-pound load and travel up to 20 miles a day!

A llama is usually gentle, but it will hiss or spit or even kick if it is ill-treated. And a llama can be stubborn. It will refuse to work if it feels too much is being asked of it.

LEARN MORE! READ THESE ARTICLES...
ARMADILLOS • CAMELS • WILD GOATS

DID YOU KNOW?

Llamas like to live in groups and will even live with sheep if there are no other llamas around. Shepherds often use llamas as "watchdogs," because llamas will fight off any animal that threatens their herd.

Which of the following do people get from llamas?
- meat
- milk
- wool
- fuel
- transportation

This llama, one of Peru's great treasures, stands in front of a man-made Peruvian treasure, the ruins of Machu Picchu.
© Blaine Harrington III/Corbis

Answer: Llamas provide people with all of these things.

Shaggy Beasts of Tibet

A yak is a heavy, strong ox with shaggy black hair and humped shoulders. Yaks and other oxen are part of the animal family that includes cattle, buffalo, antelopes, and goats. They live on the high Himalayan mountain **plateaus** of Tibet (part of China), Nepal, and Bhutan. Yaks graze on grass and need a lot of water, often eating snow in winter.

Nepalese boy leads yak.
© Nik Wheeler/Corbis

Some yaks live in the wild. But their numbers have decreased so much that soon none may be left. Bulls (male yaks) in the wild can grow as tall as six feet and may weigh twice as much as a horse. Cows (female yaks) are usually smaller and weigh less. Wild yaks live in large herds of cows, young bulls, and calves. Older bulls stay together in smaller groups.

People have also **domesticated** yaks, and these animals are plentiful. Domestic yaks are often patched black and white, and they are smaller than wild yaks. They also have longer hair than wild yaks.

In the lives of Himalayan mountain people, the domestic yak is extremely useful. People eat its meat and drink its milk. They make leather from its hide and twist its long hair into ropes and cords. Even the tail is not wasted—it is used as a fly swatter!

Because trees don't grow on the higher areas of the windy plateaus, there's very little wood available. So the yak's dried **dung** is an important fuel source to make fires for warmth and cooking. The yak is also useful for transport. Tibetans and Nepalese travel in the plateaus and mountains on the yak's back. They also use this valuable animal to carry or pull heavy loads.

LEARN MORE! READ THESE ARTICLES...
LLAMAS • PANDAS • WILD GOATS

SEARCH LIGHT

Which of the following are ways that people use the yak?
- to provide flyswatters and rope
- to supply fuel
- for milk and meat
- to carry things and people

Like the camel and the donkey in other cultures, the Himalayan yak is an extremely important beast of burden.
© Keren Su/Corbis

DID YOU KNOW?

The yak also contributes to some religious ceremonies. Butter made from yak milk provides fuel for lamps used on shrines and in certain Tibetan Buddhist celebrations.

Answer: All of these are ways people have found to make use of the yak.

Tanzania's Serengeti Plain is rich in wildlife. These male Grant's gazelles live in Serengeti National Park.
© Kevin Schafer/Corbis

DID YOU KNOW?
Gazelles have remarkable horns. Male gazelles sometimes lock horns and fight fiercely over territory.

The Bouncers

Gazelles are a graceful fast-moving kind of antelope—part of the family that includes cattle and sheep. Gazelles live on the open plains and **semidesert** regions of Africa. They're usually found in herds of 5 to 20 animals. Sometimes hundreds of gazelles move together, forming one large herd.

Gazelles are herbivores. That means they eat mainly herbs, bushes, and rough desert grasses. Some gazelles need more water than many plains animals. These gazelles often eat early in the morning or at night, when leaves contain more water than they do in the heat of the day.

Thomson's gazelle in Tanzania.
© Tom Brakefield/Corbis

Gazelles do one very unusual thing. As they travel in the herd, some of them bounce on all four legs. They keep their legs stiff, and as they hop, all four legs leave and touch the ground at the same time. It's not clear why they sometimes move this way. Perhaps they're just playing and having a good time. But there may be a more important reason for doing this. As they bounce in the air, the gazelles can see enemies moving toward the herd. The rest of the herd can then be warned of danger, and all can run to a safe place. And gazelles are swift runners.

Gazelle meat is a good source of food for people in areas where gazelles are found. The gazelle is also food for **predators** on the plains. But the population of some kinds of gazelles is shrinking because they are often overhunted for their meat. Their **habitat** is also disappearing. Desert areas are becoming drier with fewer trees, so these areas are becoming less suitable for gazelles.

LEARN MORE! READ THESE ARTICLES…
LIONS • OSTRICHES • WILD GOATS

SEARCH LIGHT

What are the two reasons for the decline in the numbers of wild gazelles?

Answer: The numbers of gazelles in the wild have declined because they are being hunted too much for their meat and because their natural habitat is disappearing.

55

Australia's Awesome Leapers

The kangaroo and its relatives are marsupials. The mother animals among most marsupials have a pouch, or pocket, attached to their bellies. The pouch is part of their furry skin. It's where the babies stay while they are nursing. Most marsupials are found in Australia and on nearby islands.

When a kangaroo is born, it's about as long as your little finger. While it's growing, it stays safe and well fed in its mother's pouch. A baby kangaroo is called a "joey."

Kangaroos visiting a golf tournament.
© AFP/Corbis

As you can see from the large photo, when the joey is big enough, it can poke its head out of the pouch. It can then eat leaves that are close enough to reach without climbing out. As it grows still bigger, it slips out of the pouch to nibble grass. Then it climbs back into the pouch at night or whenever it is tired of hopping. If there is danger while the joey is out of the pouch, the mother kangaroo picks up her baby, stuffs it into the pouch, and hops away.

Except for the small rat kangaroo and tree kangaroo, kangaroos have extremely strong back legs. The strong legs help it make the giant leaps it is known for. Its long tail helps it keep its balance while in the air. Kangaroos are herbivores, which means they eat only plants.

Kangaroos are usually gentle and timid. But if they are cornered, they'll stamp their hind feet and growl. They can grab an enemy with their front paws and kick it with their powerful back feet.

LEARN MORE! READ THESE ARTICLES...
KOALAS • OPOSSUMS • PLATYPUSES

SEARCH LIGHT

Find and correct the error in the following sentence: Kangaroos use their tails to fight.

Answer: Kangaroos use their back feet to fight.

© Wolfgang Kaehler/Corbis

DID YOU KNOW?
The word "lemur" comes from the Latin word meaning "ghost." Perhaps this is because they move about silently at night and have large mysterious eyes.

Monkeys' Primitive Cousins

Mother and baby ring-tailed lemurs.
© Kevin Schafer/Corbis

Lemurs have lived on Earth for a very long time, but they are found only in two places: Madagascar and the Comoro Islands, off the eastern coast of Africa. Millions of years ago, the island of Madagascar broke away from the continent of Africa. On the continent the monkeys were smarter than the lemurs, and the lemurs all died out. But no monkeys ever reached Madagascar, so the lemurs did well there without any competition.

The best-known species of lemur, the ring-tailed lemur, has a long striped tail, with rings of black and white. Like most lemurs, it lives in trees but looks for food on the ground. When walking on the ground, the ring-tailed lemur waves its tail back and forth, high in the air over its back. But lemurs don't hang from trees by their tails, as some monkeys do. Instead lemurs' tails help them keep their balance and sail through the air from tree to tree, like the ring-tailed lemur in the large photo.

Lemurs are mild, shy animals, but they can be very curious if there's food around. They have a better sense of smell than monkeys do, and they use it to find fruits, leaves, insects, and small birds to eat. Most of this activity takes place at night, since lemurs like to sleep during the day.

Lemurs usually have only one baby at a time. The baby clings to its mother's underside and travels with her through the treetops. After a while, the baby lemur rides on its mother's back.

LEARN MORE! READ THESE ARTICLES...
APES • CHAMELEONS • GIBBONS

SEARCH LIGHT

Which of the following statements about lemurs are true?
- They live throughout Africa.
- Lemurs live side by side with monkeys.
- Lemurs hang from their tails like monkeys do.

Surefooted Mountain Climbers

People raise goats for their milk, hair, and meat. Such goats are **domesticated**. But several types of goats live in the wild, such as the ibex, the markhor, the tahr, and the goral. Domesticated goats may have descended from these wild varieties.

The ibex is a sturdy wild goat living in the mountains of Europe, Asia, and northeastern Africa. Though ibex live in herds, old males usually live alone. The European ibex has brownish gray fur. The male has a beard and large horns shaped like half circles. Other ibex include the walia and the Siberian ibex.

Mountain goats in the Rocky Mountains of Olympic National Park, Washington, U.S.
© W. Wayne Lockwood, M.D./Corbis

The markhor is a large goat once found throughout the mountains of southern and central Asia. Now only small numbers are found, and in only a few places. The markhor is about as tall as a donkey. Unlike the ibex, its horns are long and wound like a **corkscrew**. Its coat is reddish brown in summer and long, gray, and silky in winter.

The surefooted tahr lives in herds and is usually found on steep wooded mountainsides. It can be as tall as the markhor, though it often is much smaller. Three species of tahr are found from India to Arabia. The smallest is the Arabian tahr, with its short gray-brown coat. Tahr horns are short, flat, and backward-curving.

The goral is found from the Himalayas to eastern Siberia. Its horns also curve backward. And like the ibex and tahr, it has a coarse coat that is brownish gray in color. It is smaller than these other two goats, however.

LEARN MORE! READ THESE ARTICLES...
CAMELS • GAZELLES • LLAMAS

SEARCH LIGHT

Which of the following wild goats have backward-curving horns?
a) ibex
b) goral
c) markhor
d) tahr

Ibex have dwindled in number in recent years. These male ibex stand in front of a glacier in their native Austria.
© K.M. Westermann/Corbis

DID YOU KNOW?

Mountain goats can run up nearly vertical rocks and can perch on ledges just inches wide.

G L O S S A R Y

aerialist performer who does tricks and feats above the ground or in the air

aggressive openly hostile or tending to approach with great force or energy

camouflage colors and patterns that allow a person, animal, or thing to blend in with its surroundings

canopy overhead covering

captive (noun: captivity) taken and held in a cage or as a prisoner

corkscrew device with a handle and a spiral-twist metal piece, used for removing certain bottle stoppers

crest standing clump of fur or feathers, usually on an animal's head

domestic (verb: domesticate) tame

dominant main or leading

dung animal waste

ferocious fierce and wild

flare (verb) to fan out or expand

gland structure in animals that produces special substances

habitat the physical environment in which a living thing dwells

import bring from a foreign place

larva (plural: larvae) wingless, often wormlike stage of many insects

mammal class of warm-blooded animals that feed their young with milk from special mammary glands, have an internal backbone, and are more or less covered with hair

medieval period in European history from the 5th to about the 14th century AD

mollusk animal of a group that have no backbone and are usually enclosed in a shell (for example, snails, clams, or squids)

oddity unusual thing or quality

plateau wide land area with a fairly level surface raised sharply above the land on at least one side

pollen (verb: pollinate) very fine dusty substance that comes from flowers, important in reproduction of other plants

predator (adjective: predatory) animal that lives by eating other animals

prey an animal eaten by another animal

prowl creep about in a sneaky way, often while hunting

scorpion animal of the arachnid class (which includes spiders) that has a long body and a narrow sectioned tail with a poisonous stinger at the tip

semidesert area that is much like a desert but has more rainfall

solitary alone

species group of living things that have certain characteristics in common and share a name

territorial protective of a territory or home area

tuft short mound of fur

venom poison that comes from animals